Thank you for your purchase!

I hope this book sparks your kids' imagination and creates memorable experiences. Your support is deeply appreciated!

Copyright © 2024 Lyra Lee.
All right reserved.

🌟 Author Introduction :

Hello, I'm Lyra's Dad.

Inspired by my daughter's love of activity and coloring,

I made kids' books that we can enjoy together!!

The kids' book I created is not a perfect copy.

I want children to use their imaginations to create

their own better books.

ⓘ BEFORE USING DOT MARKERS

USE A BLANK SHEET BEHIND THE PAGE TO PREVENT BLEED-THROUGH

Blank sheet

@lyra_press

DM me ✉

For any concerns, please feel free to contact me

VEHICLES WORD LIST

A

AIRPLANE   AMBULANCE

B

BICYCLE   BULLDOZER   BUS

C

CABLE CAR   CAMPER VAN   CAR   CEMENT MIXER

D

DELIVERY TRUCK   DUMP TRUCK

E

ELECTRIC CAR   EXCAVATOR

F

FERRY   FIRE TRUCK

G

GARBAGE TRUCK   GOLF CART

H

HELICOPTER   HOT AIR BALLOON

I   J

ICE CREAM TRUCK   JET SKI

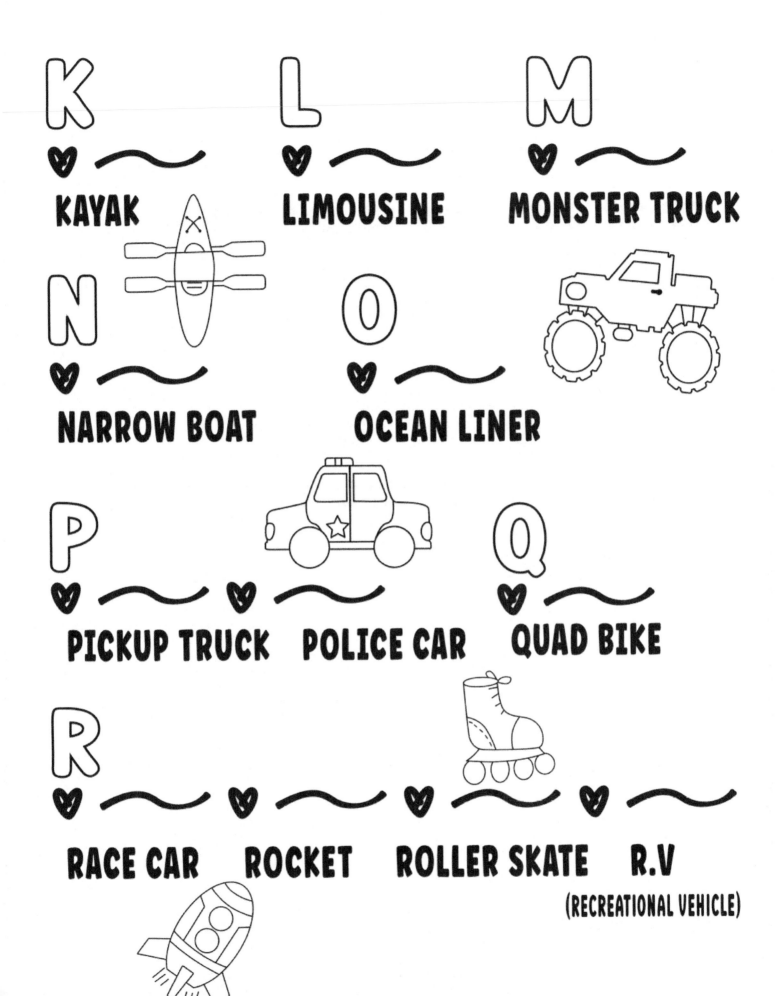

S

SCHOOL BUS SCOOTER SKATEBOARD
SPACESHIP SUBMARINE

T

TAXI TOW TRUCK TRACTOR
TRAIN TRUCK

U
UNICYCLE

V
VAN

W
WHEELCHAIR

X
SPACEX DRAGON

Y
YACHT

Z
ZEPPELIN

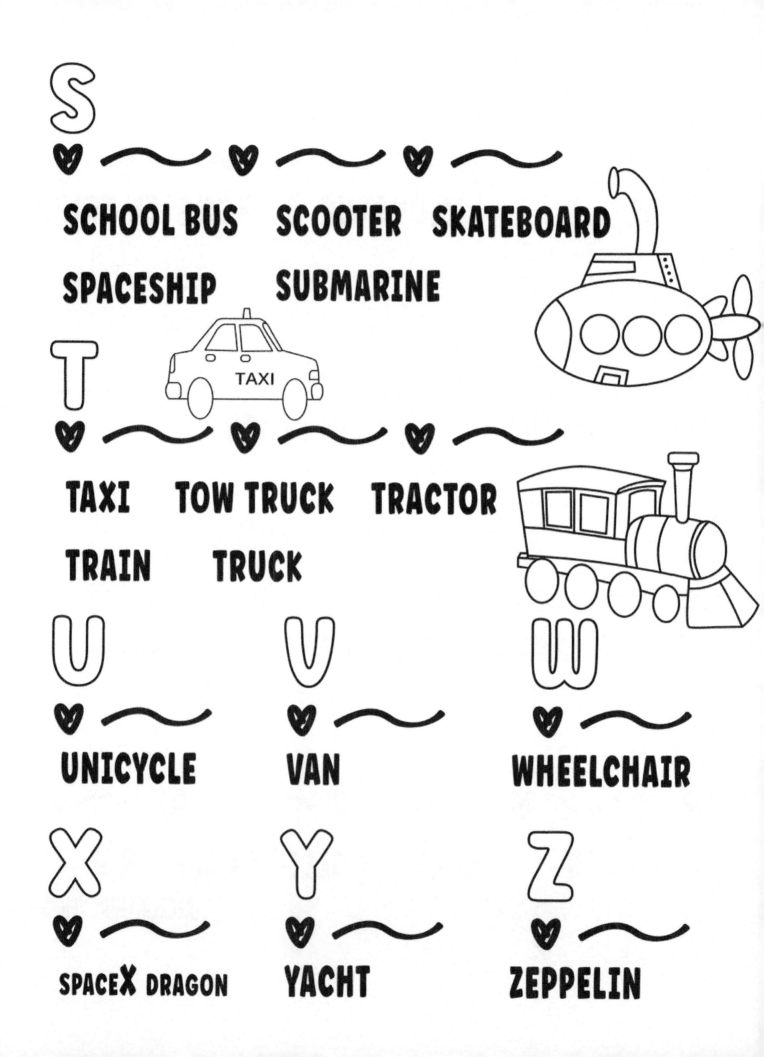

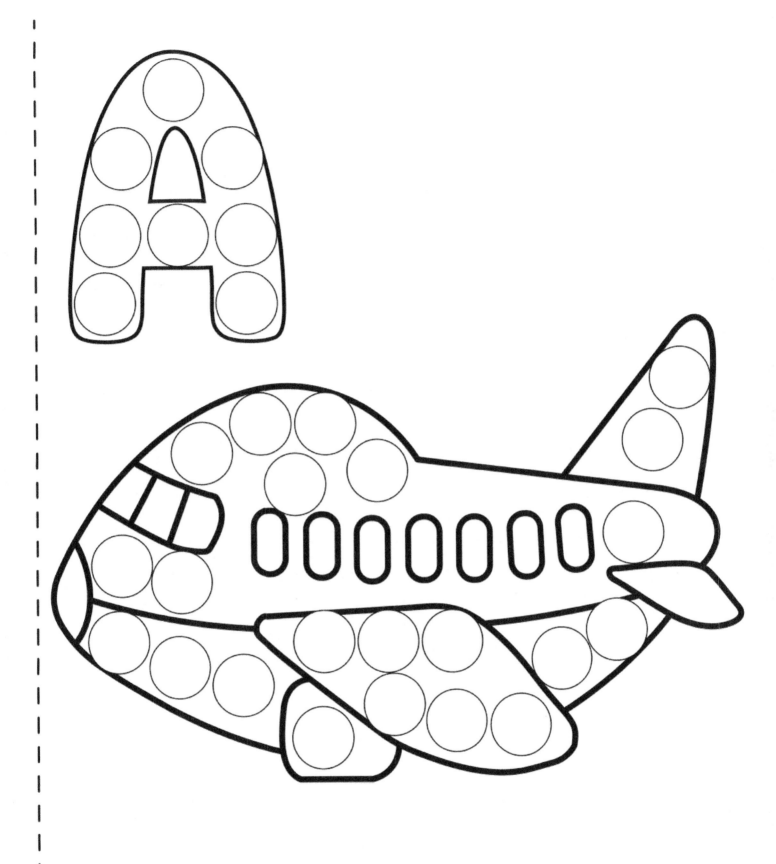

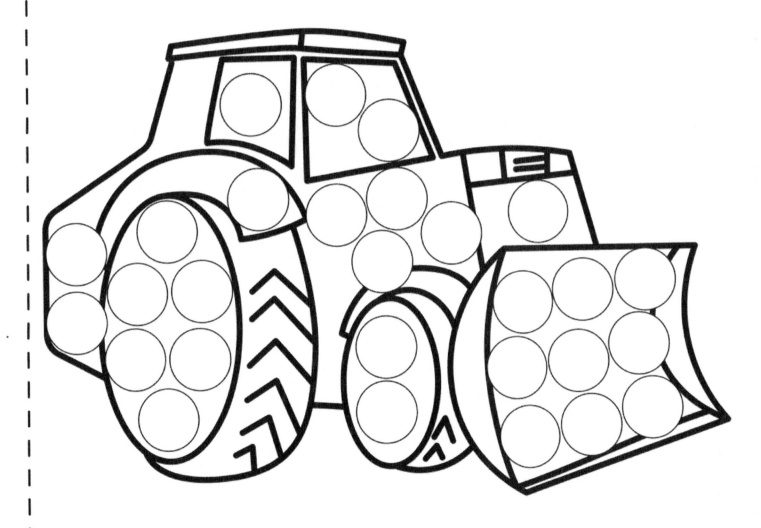
BULLDOZER

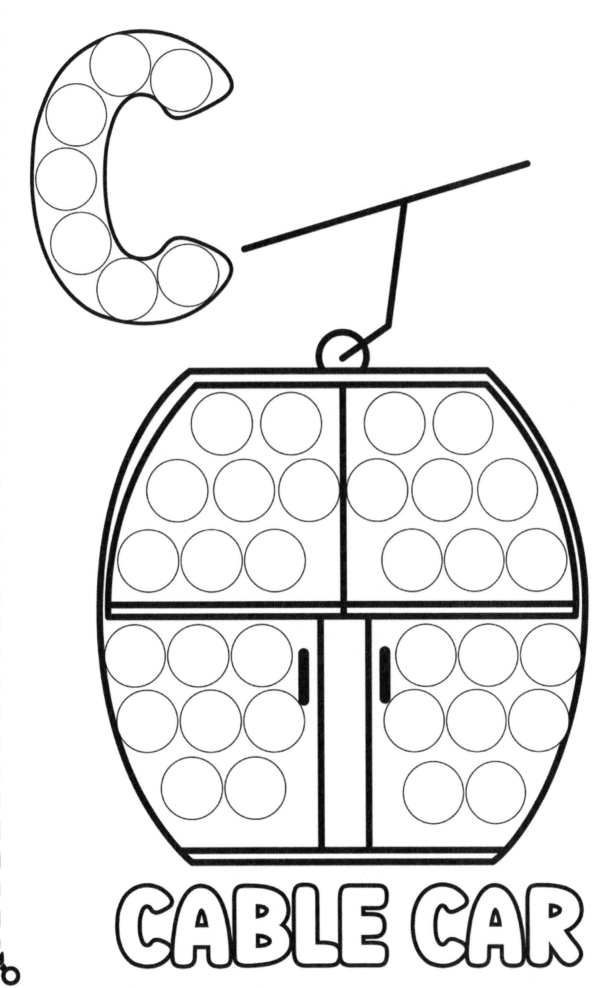

CEMENT MIXER

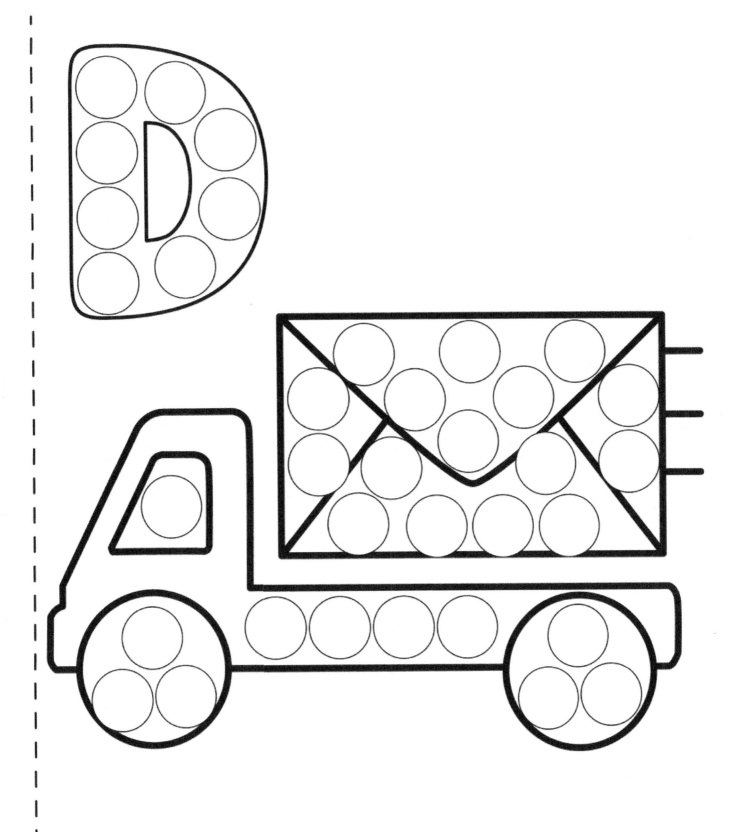

DELIVERY TRUCK

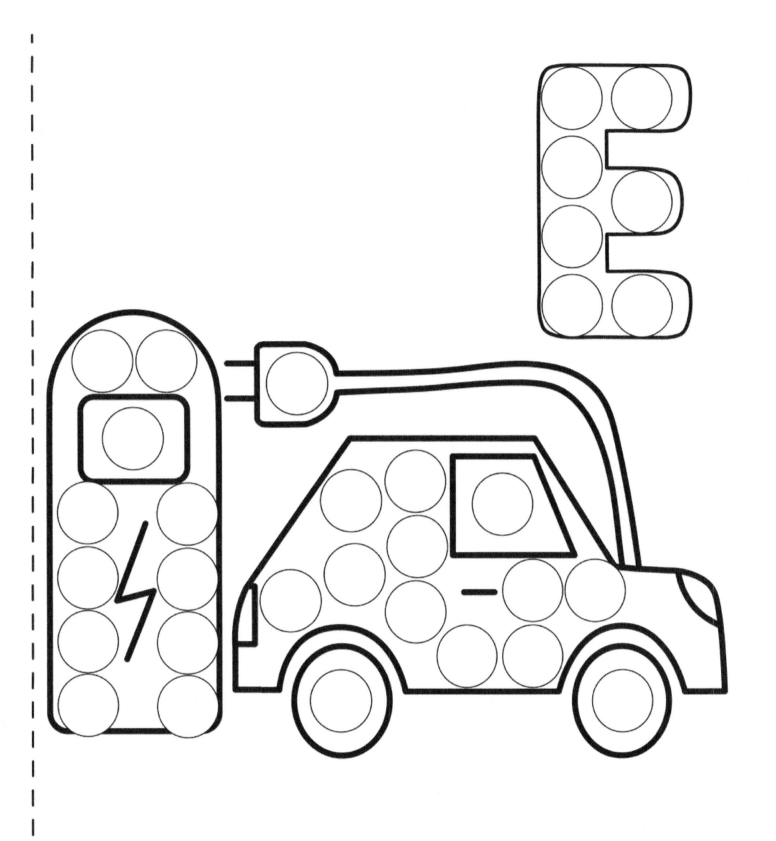

ELECTRIC CAR

EXCAVATOR

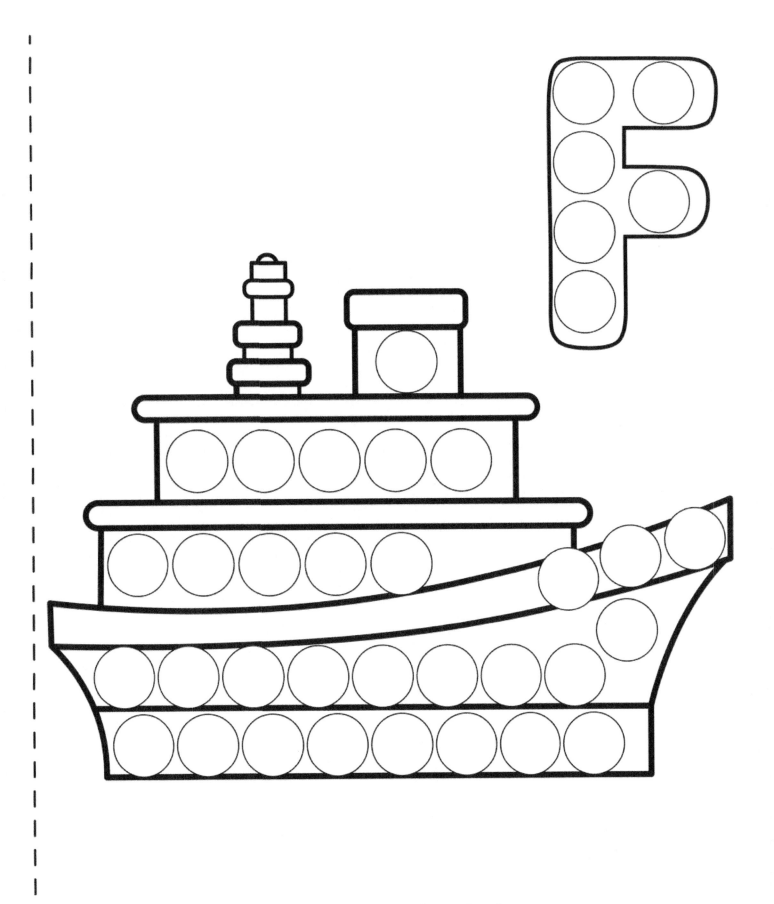

FIRE TRUCK

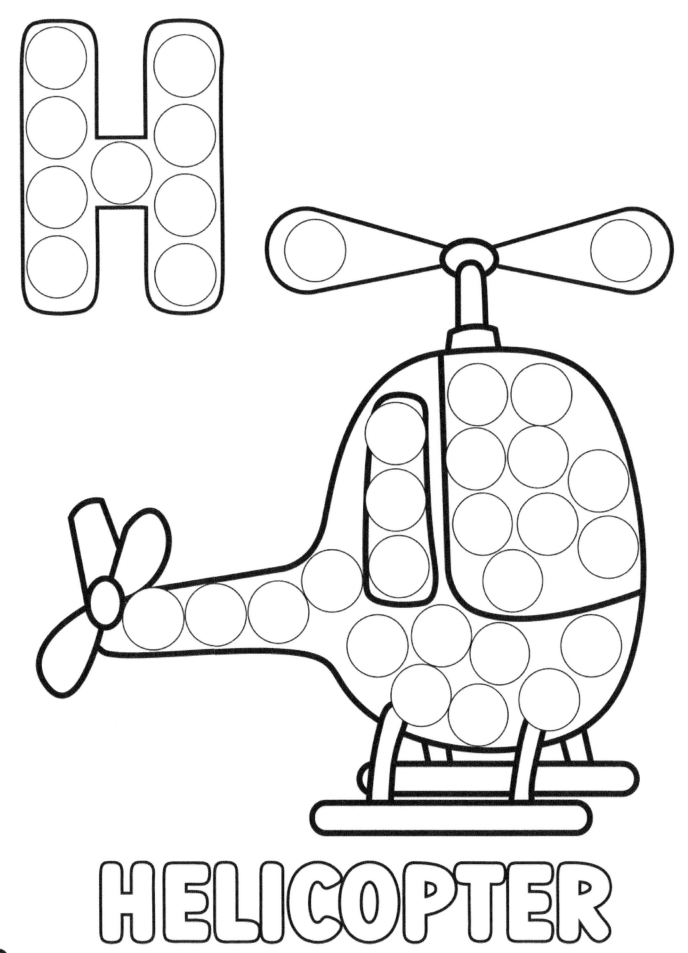

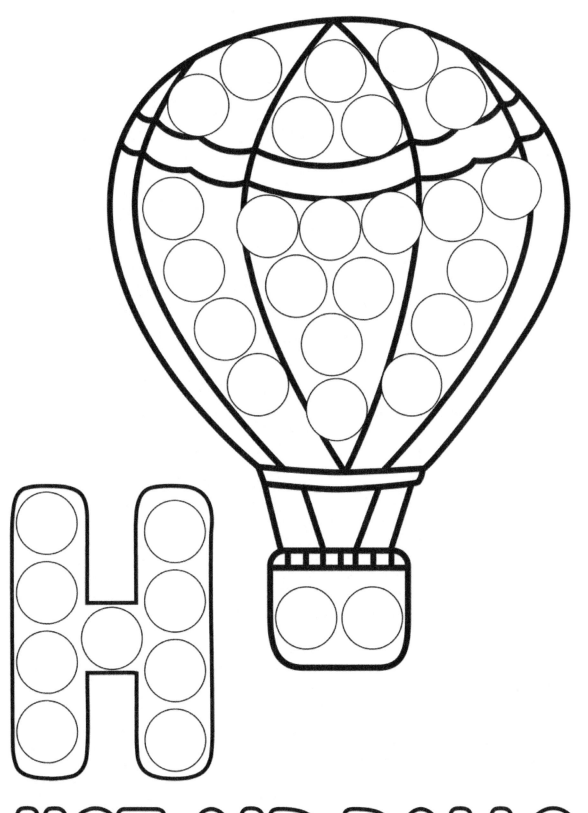
HOT AIR BALLOON

ICE CREAM

ICE CREAM TRUCK

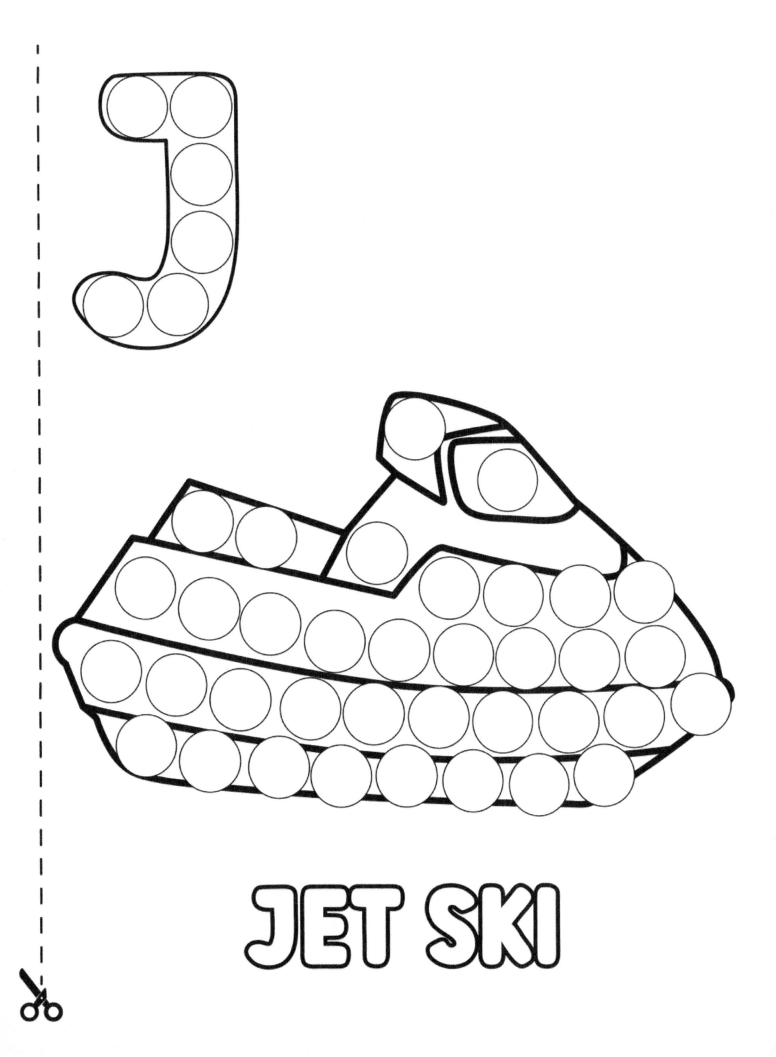

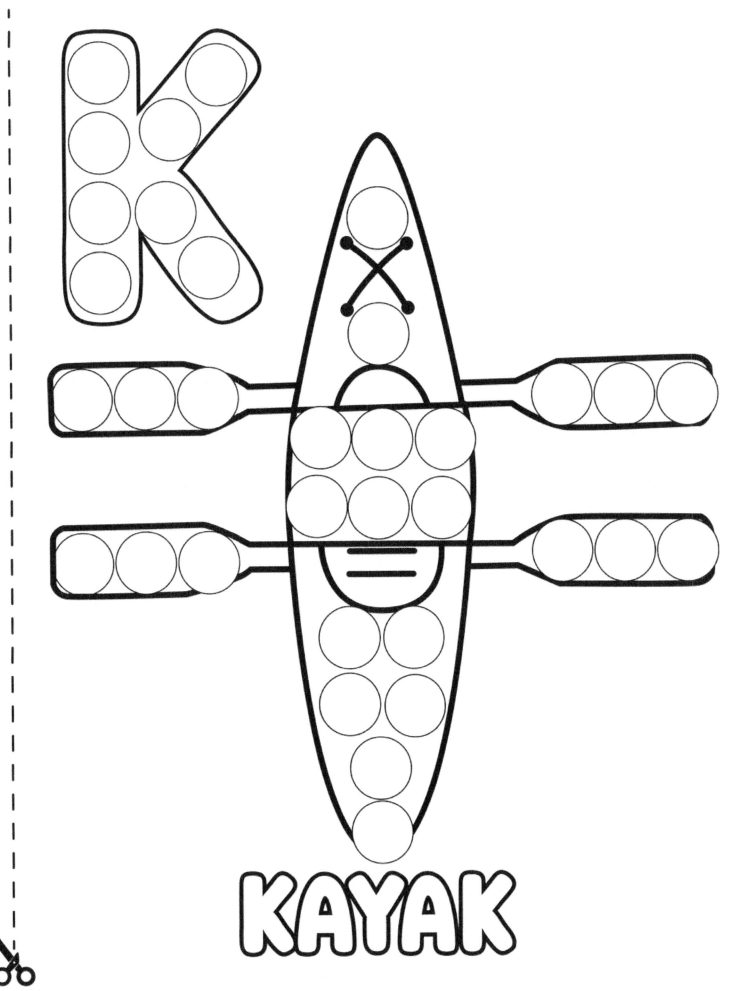

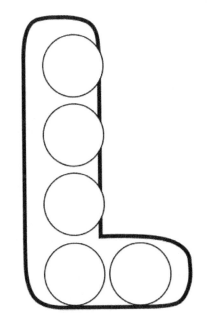

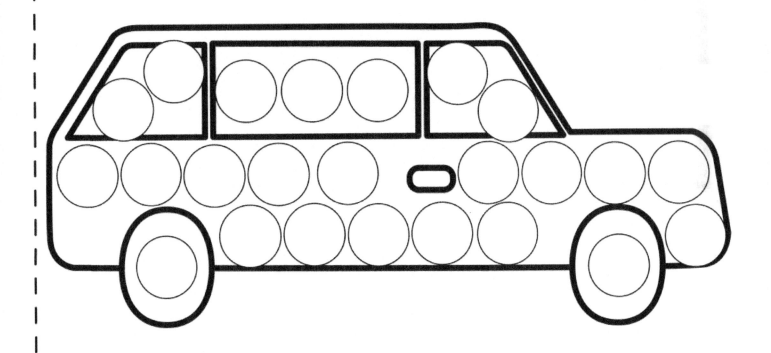

LIMOUSINE

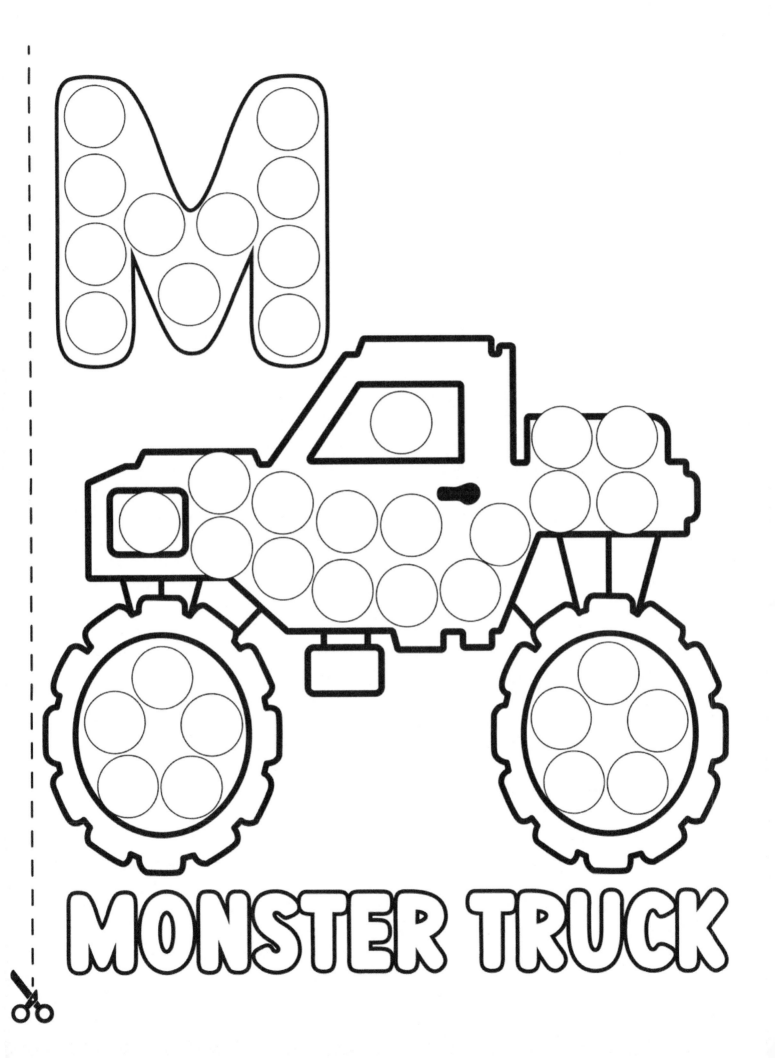

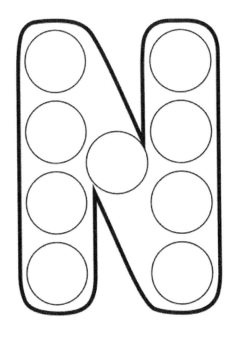

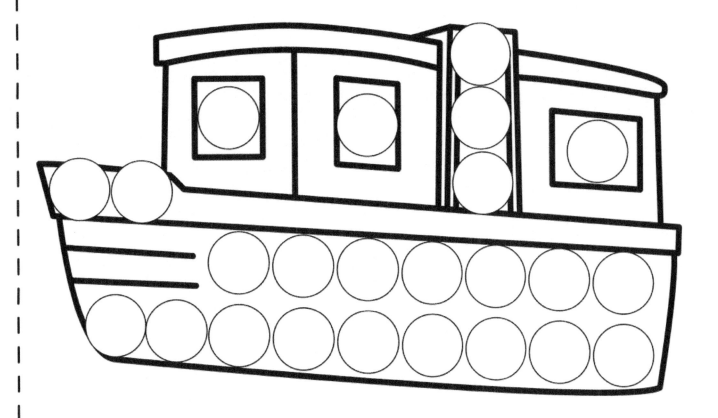

NARROW BOAT

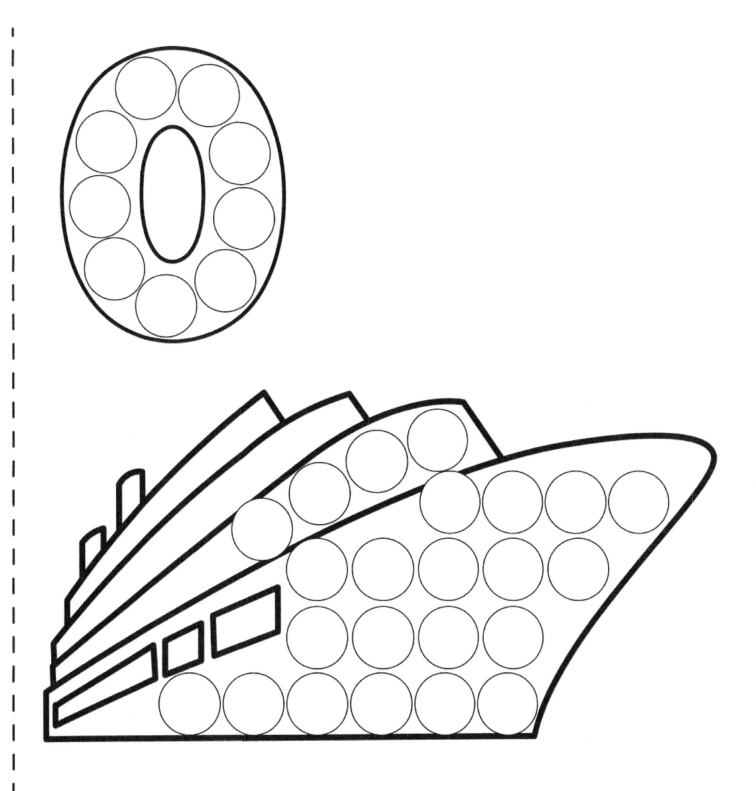

OCEAN LINER

PICKUP TRUCK

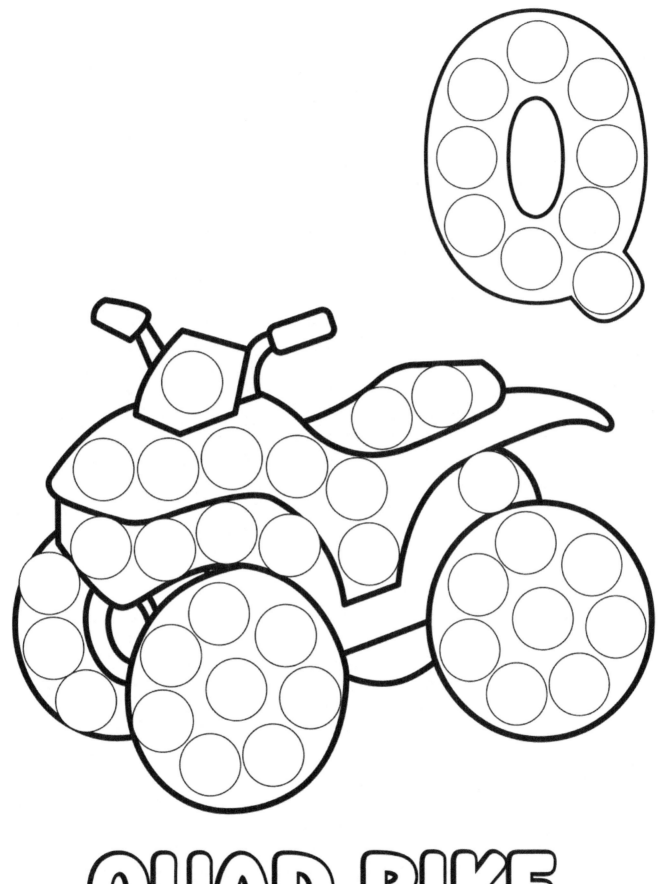
QUAD BIKE

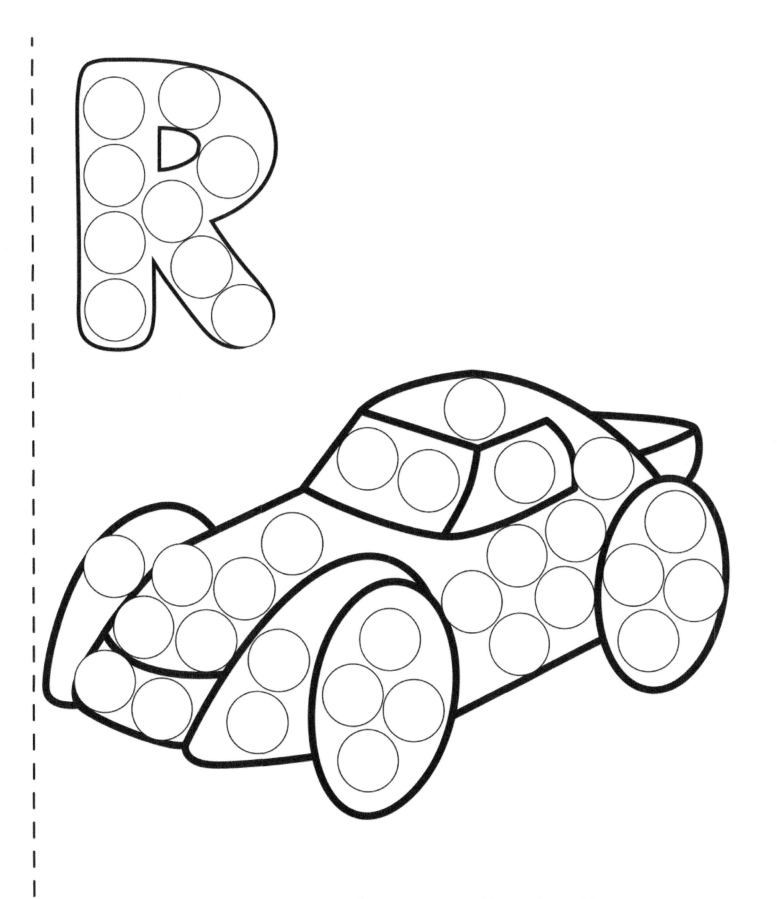

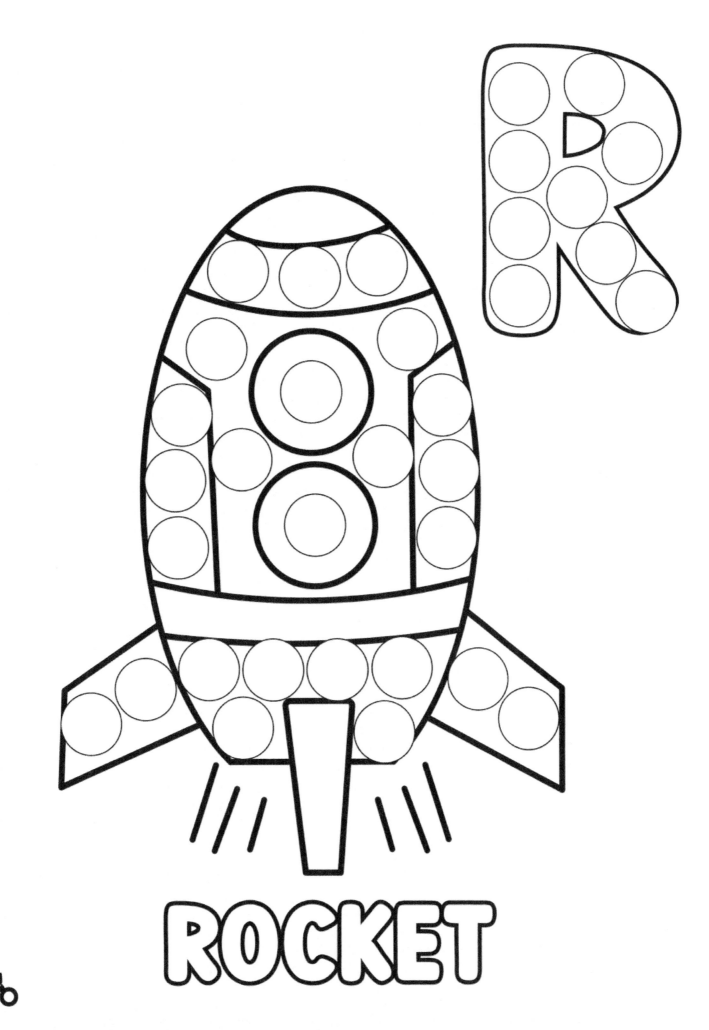

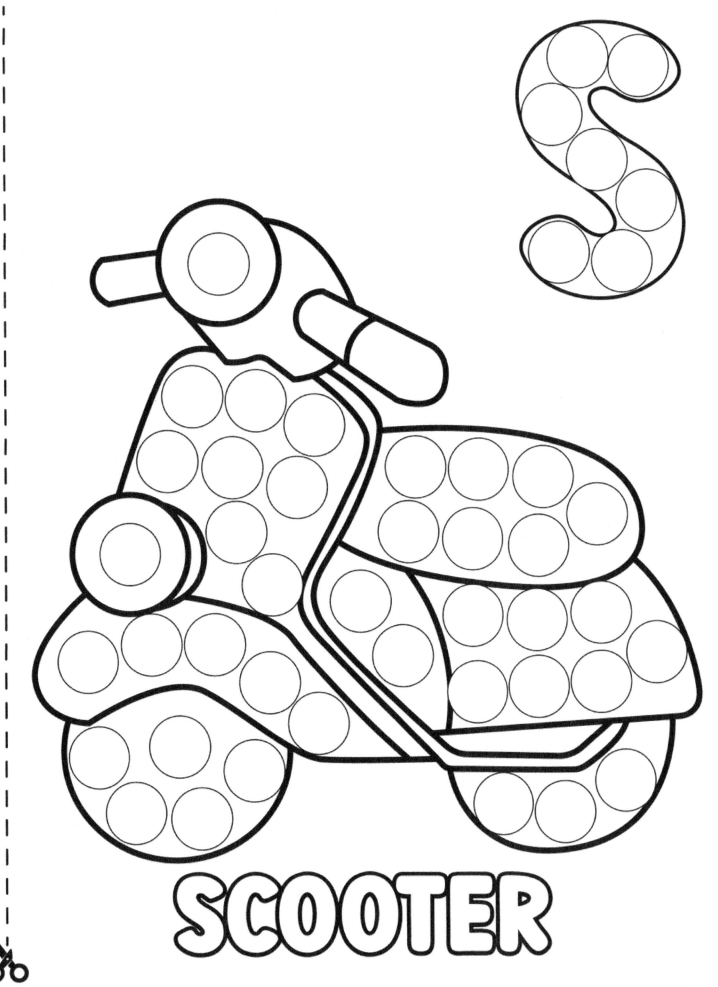

SKATEBOARD

SUBMARINE

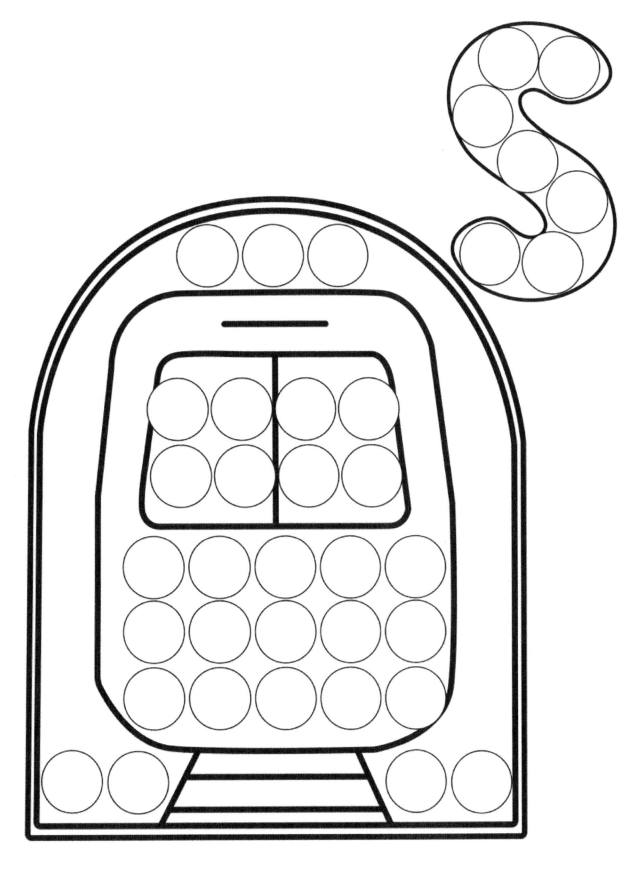

SUBWAY

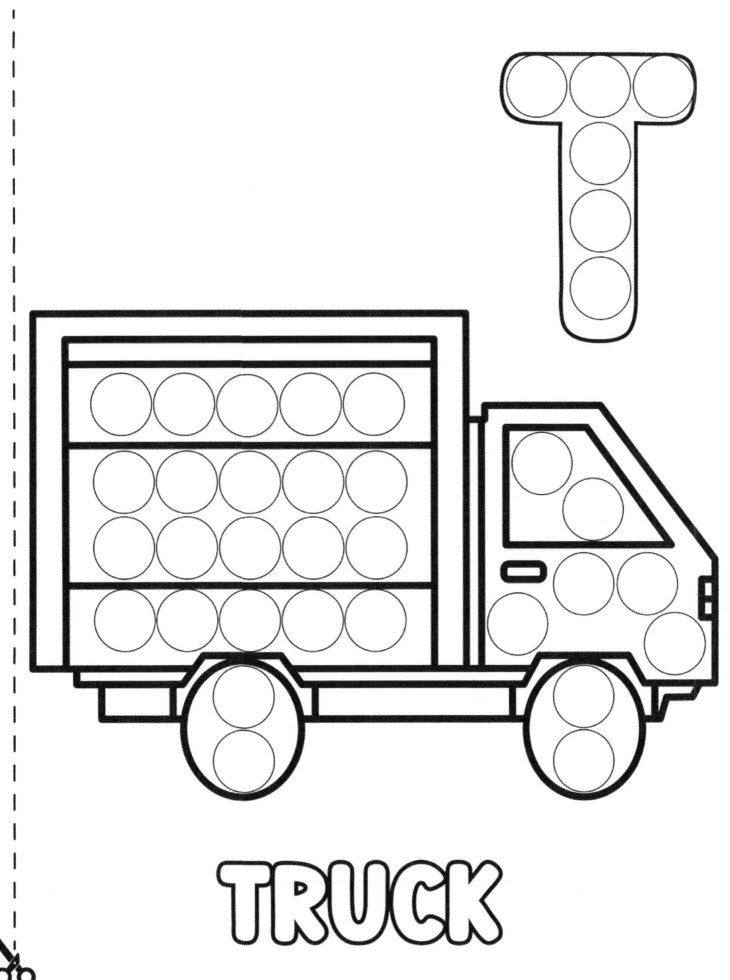

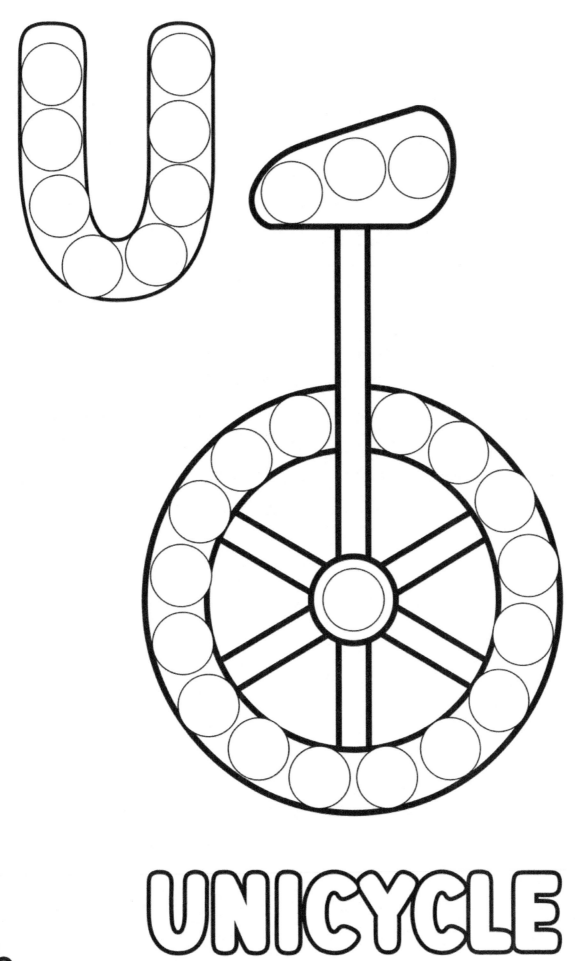

UNICYCLE

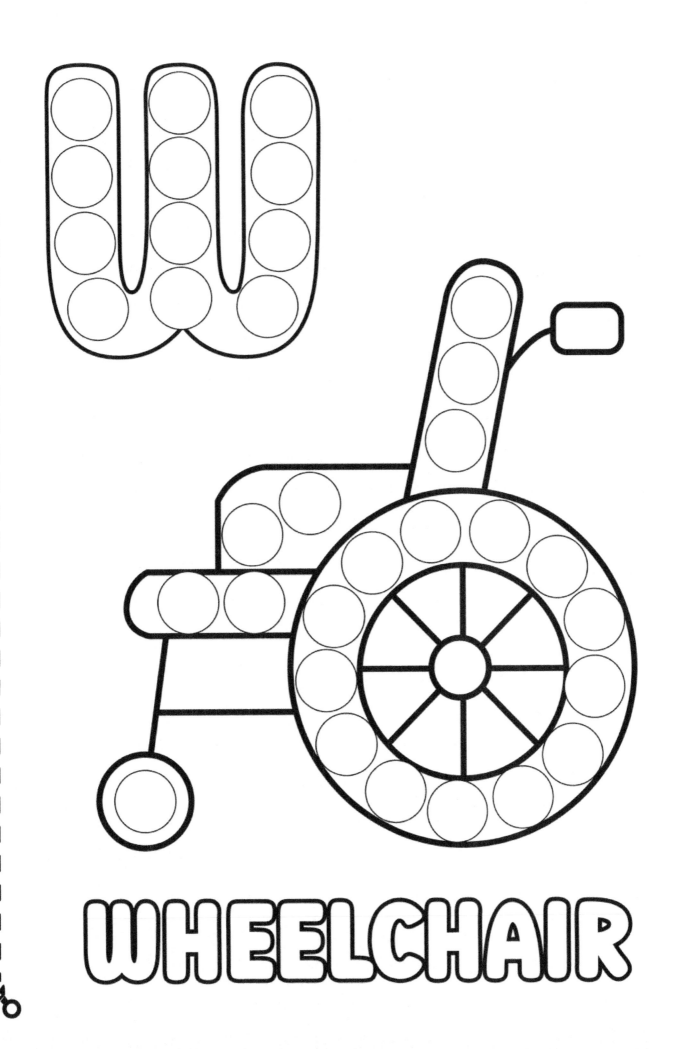

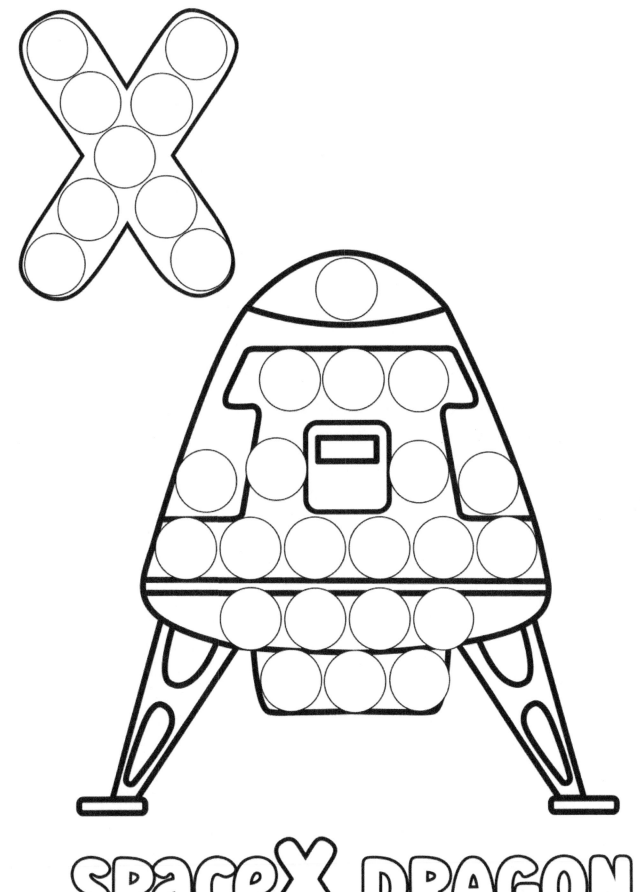

spaceX DRAGON

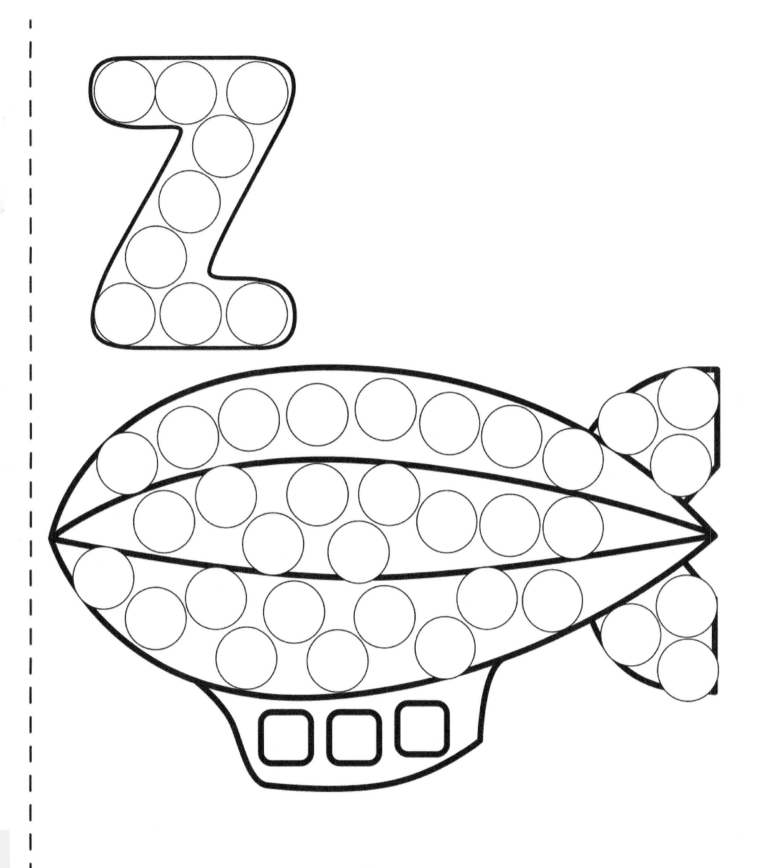

Printed in Great Britain
by Amazon